Starting Blues Harmonica

The number one method for young blues harp players

by Stuart "Son" Maxwell

AMSCO PUBLICATIONS
part of The Music Sales Group
London / New York / Paris / Sydney / Copenhagen / Berlin / Madrid / Tokyo

Note to students and teachers

1 **To get the best out of this book & CD, you will need a diatonic harmonica tuned to the key of C.** This is one of the most common blues keys, so you will get plenty of use from your harmonica. If you want to know want *diatonic* means, don't worry, you will find out later in the book.

As this book is about the *blues* harmonica, I have used the blues term "harp" in some places instead of "harmonica." It's slang, but it's the blues…

The main idea for the book & CD is to make playing the blues harp as much fun as possible. This will also help you to learn quickly, because if you are having fun then the chances are you will probably practice more. You don't have to learn to read music, but if you want an idea of how to do it, there is a bit on music theory at the end of the book.

But now, grab your harp and get ready to have fun playing the blues!

For Max and Ruby, who nearly learned to play the blues harp...

Published by
Amsco Publications
257 Park Avenue South, New York, NY 10010, USA.

Exclusive Distributors:
Music Sales Corporation
257 Park Avenue South, New York, NY 10010, USA.
Music Sales Limited
Distribution Centre, Newmarket Road, Bury St Edmunds,
Suffolk IP33 3YB, England.
Music Sales Pty Limited
120 Rothschild Avenue, Rosebery, NSW 2018, Australia.

Order No. AM 982740
ISBN 0-8256-3442-3
This book © Copyright 2006 Amsco Publications,
a division of Music Sales Corporation

Project editor: Heather Ramage
Original design: Kathy Gammon
Cover design and layout: Fresh Lemon
Photography: George Taylor
Models: Samantha Buval, Jack & George Carroll, Ruth & Natasha Collett, Lola & Harry Collins, Gemma Dodd, Emma Peat, Sarah Pughe, Alice Rosen, Ryan Shaw, Zoe Tankard, Oisín Twomey-Brenner, Evie Wilkins, Tamilori & Pelumi Obasaju

Printed in the United States of America.

Your Guarantee of Quality
As publishers, we strive to produce every book to the highest commercial standards. The music has been freshly engraved and the book has been carefully designed to minimize awkward page turns and to make playing from it a real pleasure.

Throughout, the printing and binding have been planned to ensure a sturdy, attractive publication which should give years of enjoyment. If your copy fails to meet our high standards, please inform us and we will gladly replace it.

www.musicsales.com

Contents

Note to students and teachers   2

Where the blues began   4

Introduction to the blues   5

Lesson 1: Learning to play   6

Lesson 2: Cross harp   10

Lesson 3: Wah-wah   12

Lesson 4: Riffing the blues   14

Lesson 5: Chords and effects   16

Lesson 6: Good vibes   20

Lesson 7: Blow away your blues   22

Harmonica care   25

The great harp players   26

Basic music theory   28

Last word   30

Further playing   31

Track listing and about the CD   32

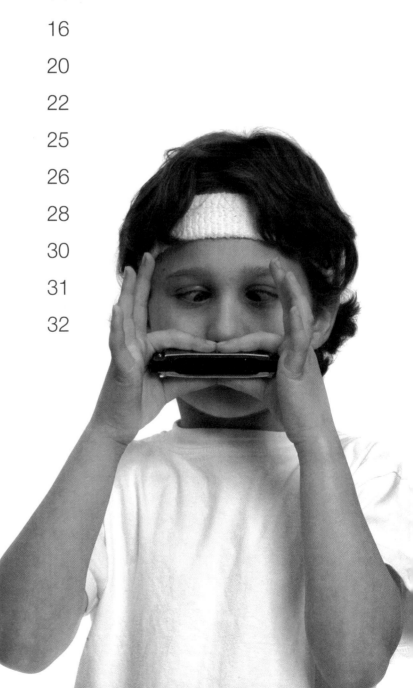

Where the blues began

If you are going to play the blues, then you have to understand where it came from. By understanding how the blues started, you can make your blues playing more powerful and much more fun.

The blues started as a music to make people feel better. It was created by slaves taken from Africa to North America during the 19th century. Lonely and frightened, the poor slaves, especially those in the southern states like Mississippi and Louisiana, made music as a way of forgetting how bad they felt so far from home. They mixed the rhythms and tunes of Africa with the songs and rhythms they heard in America and gradually the blues was born.

But whether you come from Africa, America, or any other country, the things that you make music about are the same. Love, arguments, jealousy, hard work, the funny side of life – songs have been written about these things for thousands of years. So the blues became a music loved by everyone because it was about things that everyone understands.

Originally, the blues was played on instruments like penny whistles and hand drums, because these were the only instruments available to the poor people making the music. Then, in 1896, something happened that changed the blues, music, and the world forever. M. Hohner, a maker of harmonicas, made the Marine Band, a little diatonic harmonica similar to the one you will be playing as you learn with this book.

The Marine Band was cheap, which meant that many of the blues musicians could afford to buy them. The harmonica quickly became one of the most important blues instruments. Since those early days, the blues has changed and grown. In the 1930s, when life was hard for everyone in America, many of the people living in the southern states moved north to cities like Chicago, looking for work.

They took their music with them, but in the noisy city they began to use electric instruments and microphones to make a louder sound. In the 1950s, the electric blues led to the creation of rock & roll, and rhythm & blues, from which grew nearly all the pop music that we hear today.

How to play the blues harmonica with your ears

I'm not joking. If you really want to play the blues harp, your ears are as important as your mouth and your hands. You see, if you want to get really good, you have to listen to the great harp players and hear what they played and how they played it.

In this course, we will learn to play the riffs (little patterns of music that are played over and over again in a song) and tunes that the great bluesmen created, and then how to make them our own. You don't need to play exactly like them – it's important to play your way – but you do need to learn the musical language they created, so that you can use it for your own playing.

You also need your ears to hear what is going on around you. Usually, you will be playing the harmonica in a band with other musicians. It is very important that you listen to the whole band while you are playing, so that what you play fits properly with the song.

You will find that other musicians think that harmonica players (and saxophone players, as it happens) are noisy and just interrupt everyone, even the singers. I am afraid to say that this is because a lot of harp players (yes, and sax players) do exactly that. So apart from learning to play, the most important thing to learn from this book is when NOT to play – leaving space for other musicians and making your own playing more powerful when it's your turn to shine.

Introduction to the blues

 2 **Get playing**

You can play the blues straight away. Try it. Pick up your harp and make sure you've got the low notes on the left-hand side. If your harp has numbers on it they should be on the top with the number 1 on the left.

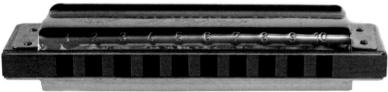

Now put your mouth over holes 3, 4 and 5 and suck gently. If you can make all three notes work, you are playing a group of notes (called a *chord*) which is known as G7. You can hear what it should sound like on **Track 2**.

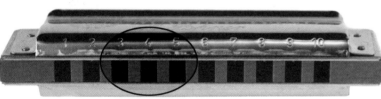

Don't worry if it doesn't sound quite right yet. With a few tries you will probably make a noise that sounds like it.

How does it sound? Do you think it is sad? Dangerous? Angry? Or even funny?

When you play the blues, you will make those notes sound like all of those things. It depends if your song is sad ("My girlfriend done left me…"), or dangerous ("I hope someone gonna start a fight…"), or angry ("You're a dirty mistreater…"), or funny ("Ain't never seen a moo cow with a saddle on it…").

That's why the blues has been around for so long and why millions of people all over the world love blues music. It can be about almost any feelings you can have inside you and, once you can make music about how you feel inside, you can usually make yourself feel better. If you can play well, you will make other people feel better too.

Keep playing

So, here you are at the beginning of the book and you can already play the blues. That's the great thing about the harp; it's really easy to start playing and sound quite good. So don't stop at G7; have another go and just try blowing and sucking, seeing how it feels and sounds.

You'll find it is easier to play the lower notes. The higher notes are made with shorter reeds (more about reeds later on page 25) so they need a bit more breath to make them work. But you should find that you don't need to blow or suck too hard, in case you choke up the note. Remember that the reeds inside are actually quite fragile and that they will break if they have to work too hard.

You might even find yourself accidentally playing a tune you recognize – it's that easy to play the harmonica. For now, however, the main idea is just to get comfortable with the harp.

Lesson 1: Learning to play

 3 Now that we have learned about the blues and got comfortable with the harp, it's time to start playing the blues properly.

Holding the harmonica

First of all, let's just check that you are holding the harmonica properly.

Hold your harmonica as shown in the picture.

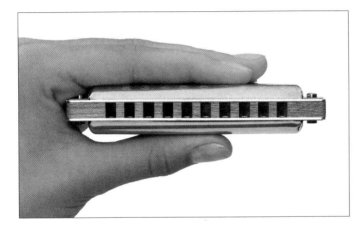

It doesn't really matter which hand you use, as long as you have a good grip on your harmonica and can put the other hand around the back to cup the sound, as shown here.

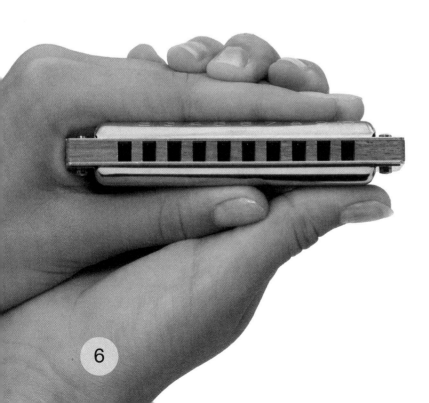

Or if you are left-handed:

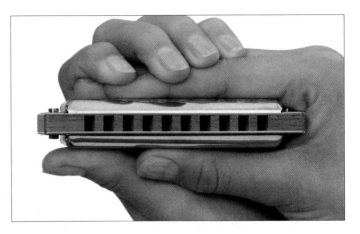

Open your cupping hand slightly to allow the sound to escape. Make sure that there is enough of the harmonica sticking out from between your fingers and thumb to allow you to get your lips well over the holes. Get comfortable, and you should have something like the harmonica grip shown below.

Blowing and drawing

4 Next, think about your breathing. You have to breathe deep, and not just suck and push the air through your lips. The proper word is *draw* rather than suck because you draw breath right down inside you; it should feel as though you are breathing with your tummy as well as your mouth and lungs.
If your cheeks and lips are doing all the work, you will quickly get tired and short of breath.

Now here's the first tune. It's a simple one, just to get you used to blowing and drawing, and moving around the harp. You will play two notes at a time; practice shaping your mouth to make sure others don't sneak in around the edges.

Notice also that I play some notes with kind of "click," using my tongue to make them sound clearer. To do this, I'm making a *duh* sound with the tip of my tongue as I blow and draw. You can use this wherever you want to make any notes stronger; sometimes I use it, sometimes I don't. It all depends how you feel.

Got you tabbed

Also, this is your introduction to our version of harmonica *tablature* or *tab* – the signs and symbols that show you how to play without having to read music.

The up arrows are blow notes: ▲
The down arrows are draw notes: ▼
The bendy arrows are bent notes (more on these in a minute): ⬇
The arrows with two heads are bends down and back up again (more later on these too): ⬍

The lines underneath tell you if it is a long note (like this: —) or a shorter note (like this: -), but use your ears to hear exactly how it should sound.

The numbers tell you which holes to blow or draw, e.g. 3-4 = holes 3 and 4 together.

The tab is divided into sections called *bars*. In music, bars help you to work out the rhythm. There is a set number of beats to count in each bar. For this book, you don't need to worry about this, since you are using your ears to get the rhythm, but the bars are useful anyway because they break the tab up and make it easier to read. I've also put in the *key* and the *time signature*; there's more on these at the end of the book (see pages 28-29).

So here we go then… Have a go at **"The Two-Timing Blues"**:

 The Two-Timing Blues

Key: **G**
Time: **4/4**
Feel: **Gentle shuffle**

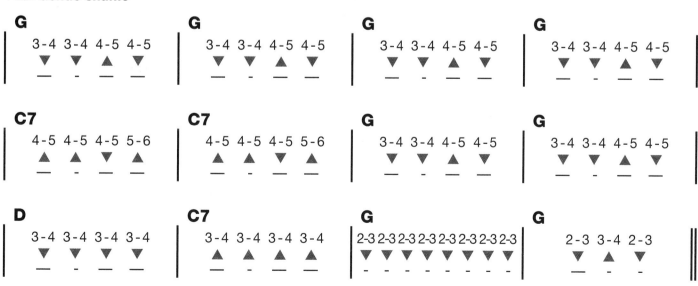

Lesson 1: Learning to play

 Single notes

Now it's time to concentrate on getting a single note. Playing one note instead of several notes together all depends on the shape and size of your mouth. You have to try by putting your lips around the harmonica until you find a shape that is comfortable and allows you to make a clean and rich single note. It's called *pursing* your lips and looks like the picture to the right.

You will have to find the shape that is right for your mouth. If the hole in your lips is too small, you will choke the note. If it is too large, you will find other notes creeping in. So keep trying, changing the shape of your lips and where you hold the harmonica until you are getting a clean single note like the one on **Track 8** – the note C played by *blowing* the fourth hole.

4
▲

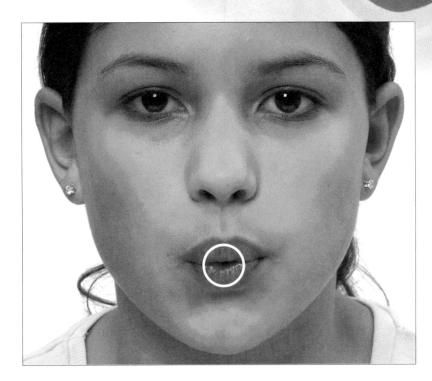

9   Bending and wailing

If you have a good note going, we're almost ready to start. There is one last thing, and it's the most important thing of all: bending the note.

If you listen to the great blues harp players, you will hear the harmonica wailing and crying as they play. These sounds are usually made by bending the reed inside the harmonica with your breath. It's not that difficult, but it's the hardest thing you will have to learn, so let's get it out of the way now.

You have been blowing a single note on the fourth hole. To start wailing, try *drawing* a single note on the fourth hole. It's the note D.

To bend the note, you have to change the shape of your mouth and tongue, so that the air comes through the harp in a different way.

Once again, it will depend on the size and shape of your mouth, so you will have to try a few times before it works.

Try curling the back of your tongue up towards the back of your mouth; your lower jaw might move forward a bit at the same time, which is fine. Also, draw in a little harder than you would usually. Keep changing the shape of your mouth until you find the note beginning to drop.

Once you've made it work, you will probably find that you can bend the note quite easily. Try gently bending and un-bending the note; it should sound like the one in **Track 9**. Remember, don't bend *too* hard because you might damage the reed.

So now here's the second tune to play. Listen to it, then have a go at playing along with it, first with the band and me, then just with the band.

10-11   The One-Note Wail

Key: **G**
Time: **4/4**
Feel: **Medium country style**

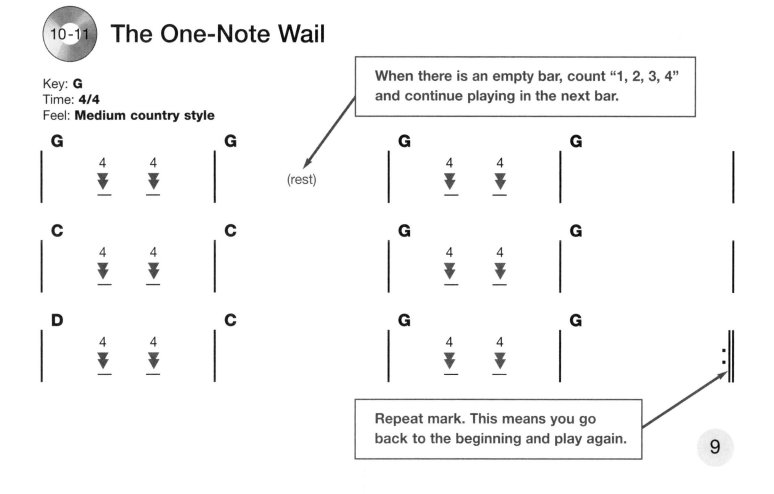

When there is an empty bar, count "1, 2, 3, 4" and continue playing in the next bar.

Repeat mark. This means you go back to the beginning and play again.

Lesson 2: Cross harp

 In this lesson, we're going to start exploring the harp a bit more and learn the most important secret of blues harmonica playing.

The secret is that you suck, or *draw*, the harmonica to get the main notes you need, rather than blowing. It's called *cross harp* and this is how it works:

Music is arranged in *keys*, which are given the same letters as the notes:

A, B, C, D, E, F, G

The key tells you which notes fit best with the

Blow: C E G C E G C E G C

Draw: D G B D F A B D F A

song. The notes in the key make a *scale*, which sounds like *do, re, mi, fa, sol, la, ti, do.*
This is called the *diatonic scale,* which is where your harmonica gets its name from; it's easy to play a diatonic scale on your harp. When you play the scale C and the *chord* C (a group of notes: C, E and G) at the same time it sounds warm and friendly, like on **Track 13.**
Have a go at playing it:

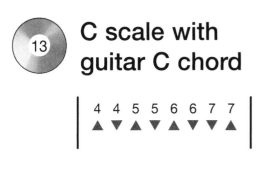

C scale with guitar C chord

4 4 5 5 6 6 7 7
▲ ▼ ▲ ▼ ▲ ▼ ▼ ▲

But to play the blues, you don't want to sound warm and friendly. You want to sound angry, sad, funny, and all those other feelings we talked about at the beginning. To do this, we have to change the notes we play and make a scale that works for the blues.

When you play a bluesy scale on its own, it sounds sad, not warm and friendly. When you play it across the C chord, it sounds different again – sad, angry, dangerous, whatever you want to make it. Listen to the two scales on **Tracks 13 and 14** to compare.

Bluesy scale in C with guitar C chord

The trouble is, you can't play this scale easily on a Marine Band or any other kind of diatonic harmonica. But if you try drawing and blowing on your C harp, rather than blowing and drawing, you can actually play in the key of G and get the blues notes you need. That's why it is called cross harp. You are playing it backwards, or crosswise, or whatever you want to call it, but you are playing the blues.

Let's try it now with a couple of examples. The first song is in the key of C, to show how warm and friendly it is when you blow a harp tuned to the same key as the song.

The second tune uses the same backing arrangement, but this time in the key of G. You play cross harp – you'll see there are lots of draw notes – and suddenly the song becomes the blues.

The Unblues – blowing across a backing track in C

Key: **C**
Time: **4/4**
Feel: **Gentle swing**

C
3-4 3-4 3-4 3-4 3-4 3-4

C
3-4 3-4 3-4 3-4

C
3-4 3-4 3-4 3-4 3-4 3-4

C
3-4 3-4 3-4 3-4

F
4-5 4-5 4-5 4-5 4-5 4-5

F
4-5 4-5 4-5 4-5

C
3-4 3-4 3-4 3-4 3-4 3-4

C
3-4 3-4 3-4 3-4

G
2-3 2-3 2-3 2-3

F
3-4 3-4 3-4 3-4

C
3-4 3-4 3-4 3-4 3-4 3-4

C
3-4 3-4 3-4 3-4

The Cross Harp Blues – drawing and blowing across the same track in G

Key: **G**
Time: **4/4**
Feel: **Gentle swing**

G
4-5 4-5 4-5 4-5 4-5 4-5

G
4-5 4-5 4-5 4-5

G
4-5 4-5 4-5 4-5 4-5 4-5

G
4-5 4-5 4-5 4-5

C
4-5 4-5 4-5 4-5 4-5 4-5

C
4-5 4-5 4-5 4-5

G
4-5 4-5 4-5 4-5 4-5 4-5

G
4-5 4-5 4-5 4-5

D
4　4　4　4

C
4　4　4　4

G
4-5 4-5 4-5 4-5 4-5 4-5

G
4-5 4-5 4-5 4-5

Lesson 3: Wah-wah

 19 You might be wondering why you have one hand cupped over the harmonica. Perhaps you've even tried moving it already, to make things louder and clearer. Well, now we're going to find out why it's there.

Back in the days when the blues began, the slaves worked on cotton plantations. Often, blowing across the flat lands of the Mississippi Delta (where the river gets wider as it reaches the sea), they would hear the whistles of trains, the cries and shouts of children, the howling of dogs and the calls of other creatures. The trains were especially sad noises – many of the slaves wished they could be on the trains north to Chicago, where they believed life was better.

When they played their blues, they would often find ways of copying the sounds. Songs about trains, like Noah Lewis's "Chickasaw Special,"

or about animals, like "Little Red Rooster," would have these sounds in them, made on their instruments.

The harp was great for this, because bending the notes, changing the shape of the mouth and moving the cupping hand could make it copy all kinds of noises.

Give it a try. Draw on hole 4 and open your cupping hand. Can you hear a change in the sound? Listen to **Track 20**. Open and close the cupping hand a few times as you draw the note and try to get that "wah" sound.

 20 ## Wah-wah on hole 4

Next, try bending the note up and down as you move your hand. You should find it really starts to wail and cry. Practice a few times, try some other holes and some chords, and then have a go at **"The Crying Blues"** and **"The Fox Chase Blues."**

 **21-22** ## The Crying Blues

Key: **G**
Time: **4/4**
Feel: **Slow blues**

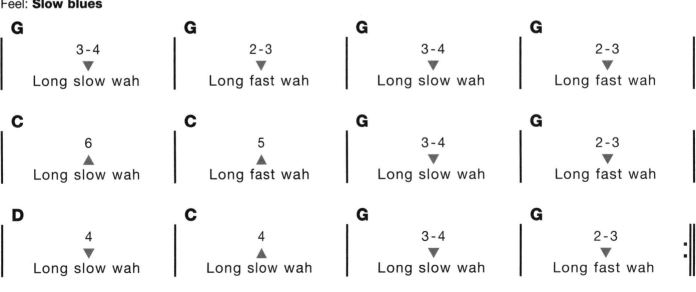

The Fox Chase Blues

Key: **G**
Time: **4/4**
Feel: **Bouncy country style**

| 2 2 2 | 3 3 3 | 2 2 2 | 3 3 3 |

| 2 2 2 | 3 3 3 | 2-3 2-3
wah wah | 1-2
wah |

| 2 2 2 | 3 3 3 | 2 2 2 | 3 3 3 |

Fine

| 2 2 2 | 3 3 3 | 2-3 2-3
wah wah | 1-2
wah |

| 4 4
wah wah | 3-4
fast wah | 4 4
wah wah | 3-4
fast wah |

| 4 4
wah wah | 3-4
fast wah | 2-3 2-3
wah wah | 1-2
wah |

| 4 4
wah wah | 3-4
fast wah | 4 4
wah wah | 3-4
fast wah |

D.C. al Fine

| 4 4
wah wah | 3-4
fast wah | 2-3 2-3
wah wah | 1-2
wah |

This means you go back to the start and stop when you come to *Fine*.

13

Lesson 4: Riffing the blues

25 This is where we really start to play the blues. In this lesson, we're going to learn about riffs. As we said before, a riff is a little phrase of notes that gets played over and over again in a song. Often, the singer sings a line and then the harp player does a little riff in reply.

There are some riffs that you just have to know if you are going to play the blues harp. They appear in countless songs, changed a bit here and there, but sounding very much like each other.

The tunes here contain two of the most important riffs; they are our versions, so if you want to copy them from a song you'll have to use your ears and make sure you play it the way it is on the record, but these are great places to start.

"The Hoodoo Blues" has a "stopping" riff in it. The idea has been used on songs like "Walking By Myself," "Hoochie Coochie Man" and even rock & roll songs like "Blue Suede Shoes."

The Hoodoo Blues

Key: **G**
Time: **12/8**
Feel: **Heavy shuffle**

28 Things get a bit trickier in **"Tumblin' Blues,"** but this is a very important riff. It is based on songs like "Rollin' and Tumblin'" and "Louisiana Blues."

 29-30 ## Tumblin' Blues

Key: **G**
Time: **4/4**
Feel: **Quick shuffle**

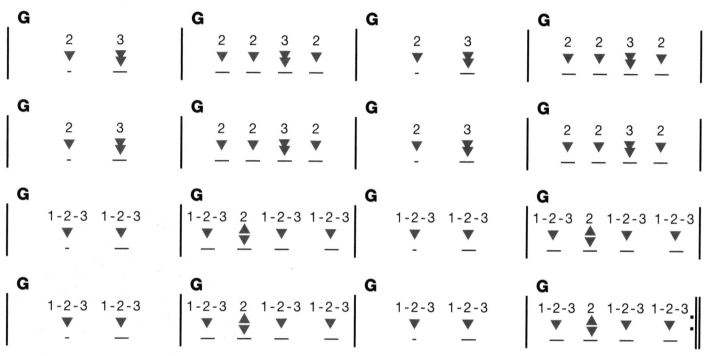

Lesson 5: Chords and effects

31 Way back at the beginning we played what I called a G7 chord, which had three notes in it: B, D and F. Whenever you play several notes at the same time, it can be called a chord. Chords are usually named after what is called the *root note,* which is the note that you start with in making a chord.

For example, the chord C contains C, E and G, and C is the root note. I cheated when I called our chord G7, because actually there's no G in the one that we played. To get the G, you would have had to draw on four holes, which is a bit hard when you are just beginning. But the sound the chord made was pretty much the same as a real G7.

As a harp player, you will have to learn a bit about chords for when you are accompanying (that is, playing along with) a singer or another instrument; you can't just keep wailing away with single notes all the time. Like nearly everything on the harp though, it's pretty easy because the notes are in the right places anyway. In fact, you've already been playing chords in the pieces we've learned so far.

What we're going to do here is practice playing chords as accompaniment and as a way of making solos more interesting.

The other reason chords are useful is because they help with sound effects. Our fox chase featured chords and in the pieces that follow we'll make train noises and chicken noises. As always, you will probably have to try changing the shape of your mouth a bit to get it to sound right; everyone's mouth is different, so you'll have to find the way that suits you best.

We'll start with chickens – roosters in fact. Bluesmen like roosters because they strut around the chicken run as though they own the place and the chickens all like them. Blues singers see them as strong, powerful figures; when you are a slave, even the life of a rooster can seem better than yours.

So here's another version of a classic blues riff, featuring rooster and chicken sounds. To make the roostery sounds, use a bit of wah-wah with your hand and try pursing your lips to change the way the note sounds. You can bend the note a bit too. For the chicken sounds, try going *duck-duck-duck* as you draw. This is the only book that will show you how to make a chicken with a duck…

32-33 Rooster Blues

Key: **G**
Time: **12/8**
Feel: **Heavy, slow shuffle**

G | 4 4-5 4-5 | **G** 4 4-5 4-5 | **G** 4 4-5 4-5 | **G** 4 4-5 4-5 |

C 3 4 3 3 3 3 | **C** 3 4 3 3 3 3 | **G** 4 4-5 4-5 | **G** 4 4-5 4-5 3 4 |

D 4 4-5 4 3 2 | **C** 3 3 3 3 3 3 3 3 | **G** 2 2 2 2 2 2 2 2 2 | **D** 2 4 4 |

G 4 4-5 4-5 | **G** 4 4-5 4-5 | **G** 4 4-5 4-5 | **G** 4 4-5 4-5 |

C 3 4 3 3 3 3 | **C** 3 4 3 3 3 3 | **G** 4 4-5 4-5 | **G** 4 4-5 4-5 3 4 |

D 4 4-5 4 3 2 | **C** 3 3 3 3 3 3 3 3 | **G** 2 2 2 2 2 2 2 2 2 | **G** 2 2-3 2-3 |

⭐ **TIP** Always remember to move the harmonica across your mouth – don't move your head – it's far less accurate. If you think you're having trouble with this, try practicing in front of a mirror.

Lesson 5: Chords and effects

 In our next song, we're into one of the most important harmonica sound effects: the train. We use chords to make the sound of the steam engine (there were no diesel-powered trains back when the blues began).

We've also got our duck back, this time making a chug-chug sound.

Chords are also needed to make the sad sound of the whistle, echoing across the plantation, or back down the track to the poor man waving goodbye to his girlfriend. You'll need to bend a bit too, to get that real crying sound.

 **Train Gone Blues**

Key: **G**
Time: **4/4**
Feel: **Bright country bounce**

Introduction   *Repeat introduction four times*

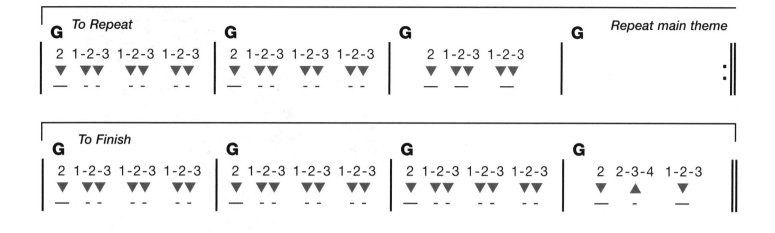

G *To Repeat*
2 1-2-3 1-2-3 1-2-3

G
2 1-2-3 1-2-3 1-2-3

G
2 1-2-3 1-2-3

G *Repeat main theme*

G *To Finish*
2 1-2-3 1-2-3 1-2-3

G
2 1-2-3 1-2-3 1-2-3

G
2 1-2-3 1-2-3 1-2-3

G
2 2-3-4 1-2-3

---

37 "Chicago Blues" is based on the style of blues that came from the city of Chicago, where the blues players first began to use electric guitars, microphones and amplifiers.

You are not playing the tune here – it's the piano that has the lead – but you are playing along with chords that fit the music.

There's also a new effect here: the *trill*. You'll hear it all over the blues songs you listen to. To play a trill, move the harp quickly from side to side in your mouth, so that two holes next to each other make the trill.

38-39 # Chicago Blues

Key: **G**
Time: **12/8**
Feel: **Heavy shuffle**

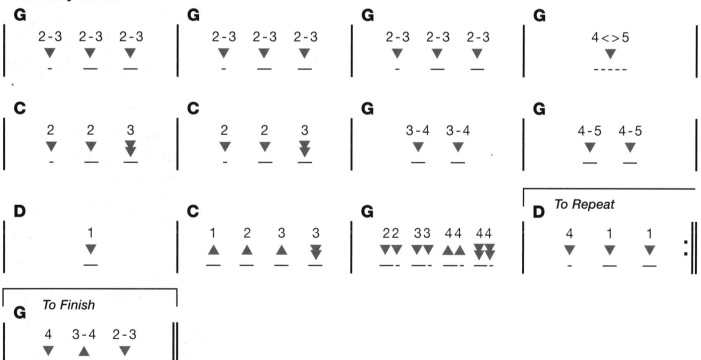

G
2-3 2-3 2-3

G
2-3 2-3 2-3

G
2-3 2-3 2-3

G
4 < > 5

C
2 2 3

C
2 2 3

G
3-4 3-4

G
4-5 4-5

D
1

C
1 2 3 3

G
22 33 44 44

D *To Repeat*
4 1 1

G *To Finish*
4 3-4 2-3

Lesson 6: Good vibes

40 I'm going to get fussy now. Have you noticed how some singers always have a wobble in their voice, where they kind of bend the note up and down a bit? It's called *vibrato* and opera singers do it a lot. I have to say it drives me nuts if they do it too much. But this is not opera and in fact, vibrato is an important part of the blues. Used in the right way, it can really add power to your playing. And by the right way I mean NOT TOO MUCH!

To get the vibrato, you just need to bend the note down and back up again quickly. Use exactly the same mouth shape as you do for a bend, but just change it backwards and forwards quickly. You might already have tried it anyway. The main thing is to notice how it's only used in a few places. Also, don't do it too hard, because you might weaken the reed inside the harp.

41 There's another type of wobble where the note gets louder and softer very quickly, which I call *tremolo.* This is an effect that makes the music more moody and tense – darker, if you like.

Tremolo is a bit harder, because it has to come from right down in your tummy. You have to draw your breath in little jerks: try going *uh-uh-uh* right at the back of your throat – further down, if you can. This will need quite a bit of practice, unless it just happens to work for you.

We're going to have a go at both, using **"The Moody Blues,"** which is based on a song called "Mighty Long Time" by the greatest blues harmonica player of all, Sonny Boy Williamson II.

42-43

The Moody Blues

Key: **G**
Time: **4/4**
Feel: **Slow, dark blues**

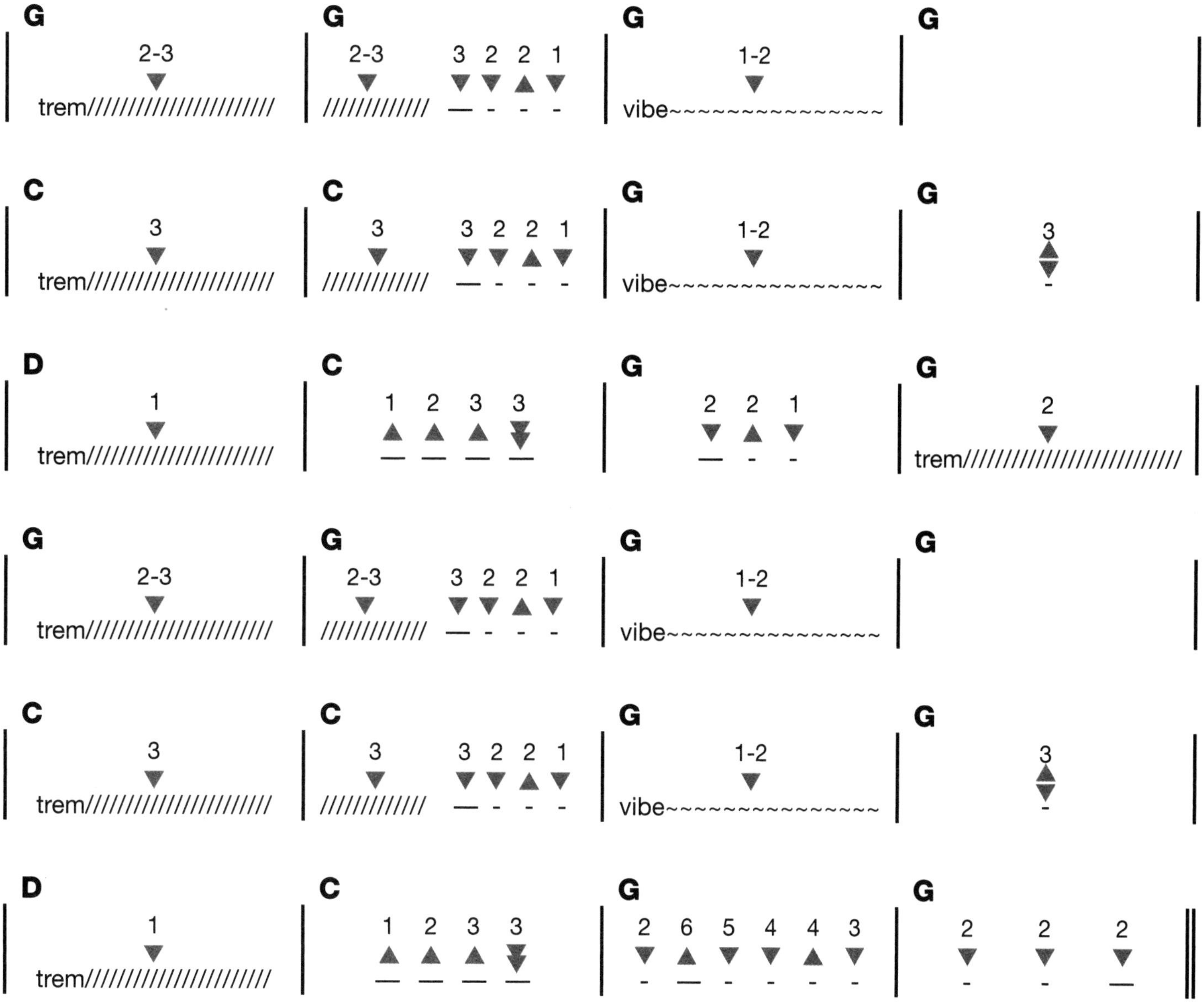

TIP **Stay relaxed and let your breathing be deep, free and easy. Try taking a few good, slow, deep breaths before playing, to get your lungs ready.**

Lesson 7: Blow away your blues

44 This is the last lesson and it's just a bit of practice playing really. The idea is to help you to start *improvising* on the harp. Improvising means making it up as you go along, instead of playing a tune that someone else has written. It is the bit where you break free from written music and start to make music out of nothing, the way you want to play it.

Learning to improvise means using your ears more than ever. You have to listen to the rest of the music and play notes and phrases that fit with it.

The magic of improvisation is that the further you get from the tune, the more chance there is of something amazing happening in the music. When you get a group of musicians all improvising away like mad, you can sometimes get a lot of noise, but you can also get some really exciting music.

Improvisation is a big part of blues playing and the only way to learn it is to practice, practice, practice. You can start off by copying some of the simpler bits that I'm playing on the tracks and then gradually add your own bits onto them. The more bits you add, the less room there will be for the bit you started with until you are not playing it at all – it's all you.

Also, remember as you play along (it's called *jamming* in blues language) to let the other musicians in the band have their turns as well. When the piano and the guitar are playing their solo bits, you must stop playing or find little chords to accompany them that won't interfere with what they are doing.

So here we are: four classic blues styles for you to play with until you are out of breath.

45-46 City Blues Jam

Key: **G**
Time: **12/8**
Feel: **Quick shuffle**

22

Midnight Blues Jam

Key: **G**
Time: **4/4**
Feel: **Slow blues**

Dm6

4	5	4	3
▲▼	▲	▼	▼

Gm6

6	5	5	5
▲	▲	▼	▲

Dm6

4
▼

Dm6

Gm6

6	5	5	3	2
▲	▼	▲	▼	▼

Gm6

6	5	5	4	2
▲	▼	▲	▼	▼

Dm6

3
▼

Dm6

4	5	4
▼	▲	▼

Am6

5	5	4	5	4
▼	▲	▼	▲	▼

Gm6

6	5	5	4	5	3
▲	▼	▲	▼	▲	▼

Dm6   Gm6

2	3	4	4	5	6
▼	▼	▼	▲	▲	▲

Am6

6	5	4
▲	▼	▼

Swinging Blues Jam

Key: **G**
Time: **4/4**
Feel: **Swinging blues**

4	5	4	5
▼	▲	▼	▲

G

6	6	4	5	4	5
▲	▲	▼	▲	▼	▲

G

6	6	4	5	4	5
▲	▲	▼	▲	▼	▲

G

6	6	5	5	4	5	3	2
▲	▲	▼	▲	▼	▲	▼	▼

G

4	5	4	5
▼	▲	▼	▲

C

6	6	4	5	4	5
▲	▲	▼	▲	▼	▲

C

6	6	4	5	4	5
▲	▲	▼	▲	▼	▲

G

6	6	5	5	4	5	3	2
▲	▲	▼	▲	▼	▲	▼	▼

G

4	5	4
▼	▲	▼

D

5	5	5	4	5	4
▼	▼	▲	▼	▲	▼

C

6	5	5	4	5	3	2
▲	▼	▲	▼	▲	▼	▼

G

2	2	2	2	2	2
▼	▼	▼	▼	▼	▼

G

2	1	1
▼	▼	▼

Lesson 7: Blow away your blues

 51-52 Rocking Blues Jam

Key: **G**
Time: **12/8**
Feel: **Rocking blues**

Harmonica care

To get the best out of your harp, it's good to know how it works. Here's a quick guide, with some tips on care for your harp.

The harmonica is a *free reed* instrument. The sound comes from little strips of metal, or reeds, attached to a metal plate which is fixed onto the body of the harp, over the holes. There are two reeds for each of the ten holes in a diatonic harp, ten on the top, ten on the bottom. It's called a free reed instrument because the sound is made by the reeds vibrating in the air; in ordinary reed instruments, like saxophones or clarinets, the sound is made by the reed vibrating against something. When you blow, the top reeds open and the bottom reeds close into their holes. When you draw, the bottom reeds open and the top reeds close up. It's as simple as that.

The reeds themselves are particularly delicate and it is important to keep them clean. Playing a harmonica can be messy, so you should always tap the stuff out of your harmonica before you put it away (see pictures).

Also, it makes sense not to eat anything just before you are going to play, and drink only water while you are playing; soda, potato chips, nuts and other things are not good for your harp.

If you find that some notes are not working properly you can, with care, gently lift the top and bottom covers off the harmonica to see the reed plates. Carefully check that the reeds are sitting neatly in their slots and that they are clean, with nothing to stop them from opening and shutting properly. You can clean them with a damp cotton swab, but take care not to leave any bits of cotton behind.

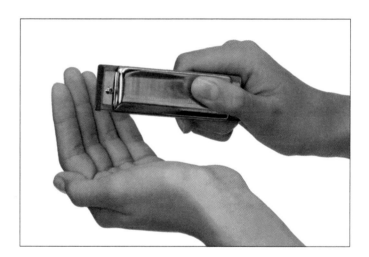

The great harp players

To play harmonica with your ears, you have to have something to listen to, so here are a few people who have made the blues harp one of the great sounds of modern music. Listen to these players, learn to play their riffs and then mix them in to your own style. It's all part of learning the language of the blues, so that when you get up on stage with a blues band and they say "Louisiana Blues, in A," you'll know what to do…

Sonny Boy Williamson I

John Lee Williamson was the first harp player to achieve lasting national fame in America. He was recording from the late 1920s until 1948, when he was murdered on his way home from a *gig* (blues, jazz and rock word for a concert). His style was very popular and most of the harp players that came after him sounded a bit like him. Two important songs of his are "Good Morning Little Schoolgirl" and "Bring Another Half Pint."

Sonny Boy Williamson II

People argue over whether Rice Miller stole John Lee's Sonny Boy name, or John Lee stole his; certainly John Lee was the first famous Sonny Boy. But this Sonny Boy is a true master and, for many harp players (including me), the greatest of all. Notice how he plays only a few notes; it's all in the timing and the way he plays them. Nearly all Sonny Boy tracks are important but you MUST listen to "Mighty Long Time," "Help Me" and "Bring It On Home."

Sonny Terry

Did I mention you must change your name to Sonny before you can play blues harp? That's why I get called Son Maxwell – I'm not quite up there with the Sonnys yet… Anyway, Sonny Terry was the greatest harp player in the country style. He was blind and worked with other famous bluesmen like Brownie McGhee and Blind Boy Fuller and he was a master of special effects, as well as a wonderful soloist and accompanist. Listen to his "Fox Chase" solo and his version of "Key To The Highway" with Brownie McGhee. And I was joking about changing your name.

Little Walter

This magnificent player made the amplified harmonica sound famous, using special effects like echo and distortion to change the sound of his harp. Essential tracks include "Juke," "Blue Light," and "Louisiana Blues," where he accompanies the great blues singer Muddy Waters.

Big Walter Horton

You could also change your name to Walter, I suppose. This harp man is slightly less well-known than the others, but I think he is every bit as good. He also worked with Muddy Waters, and with Jimmy Rogers, with whom he played some of his best solos. Look out for "Easy" and "Walter's Boogie."

Other great players

There are far too many to include all of them, of course, but look out for Noah Lewis and Carey Bell, as well as white bluesmen like Paul Butterfield, Paul Jones, Charlie Musselwhite and Ron "Pigpen" McKernan of the Grateful Dead. You should also listen to Tony "Little Sun" Glover, who worked with "Spider" John Koerner and Dave "Snaker" Ray in Koerner, Ray & Glover.

Basic music theory

Harmonica players who know which notes they are playing are quite rare and as a blues player you probably won't need to know much. But it is very useful to understand the basics of music theory, just so you can at least know what the guitarists and piano players are talking about. So here's a very quick introduction to the basics of reading music:

Beats and notes

This is a staff, which is made up of five lines called staff lines.

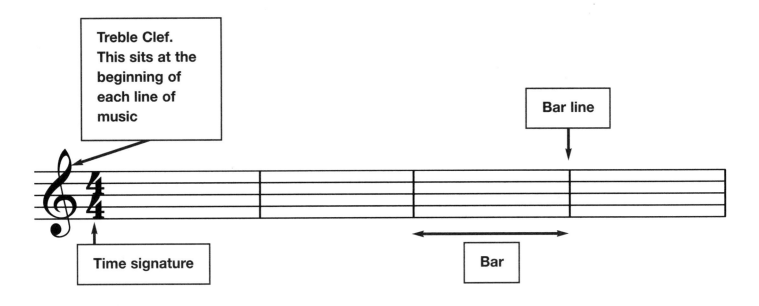

Treble Clef. This sits at the beginning of each line of music

Bar line

Time signature

Bar

The position of the note on the staff tells you how high or low the note is:

C D E F G A B C

There are lots of different types of notes.
They tell us how long to play for:

 **Quarter Note**

One quarter note equals one count.

 Whole Note

Equals four quarter notes – play the note for four counts.

Half Note

Equals two quarter notes – play the note for two counts.

 **Eighth Note**

Equals half a quarter note – play the note for half a count.

 **Sixteenth Note**

Equals a quarter of a quarter note – play the note for a quarter of a count.

Time signature

The staff in the example on page 28 is divided into sections called *bars*. These are separated by *bar lines*. Bars are needed to help show the *rhythm* of the music. Rhythm is measured by the number of beats in a bar. The rhythm used for a piece of music is known as its *time signature*.

The time signature of each piece of music tells you how to count the number of beats. The most widely-used time signature is **4/4**, which means that there are four beats in the bar, each worth a quarter note.
The top figure gives you the number of beats, the bottom or lower figure tells you what each beat is worth – a half note, quarter note, eighth note and so on.

In this book, we have used 4/4 and **12/8**, which means there are 12 half beats in the bar. You count 12/8 in little groups of threes – 1-2-3, 1-2-3, 1-2-3, 1-2-3 – to get the kind of shuffle rhythm used in hundreds of blues songs.

That's about as much as you need to know about music theory for now; there is a bit more on the subject in my other book, *The Complete Harmonica Player* (Order No. AM 977438), which is also published by Amsco Publications. It includes a CD that features examples of different time signatures.

Last word

(53) On the CD I'm joined by the other members of the band that I play with, Storm Warning. They are Bob "Mad Dog" Moore on guitar, Derek White on the bass, Ian Salisbury on the keyboards and Roger Willis on the drums. You can find out more about us at our Website, **www.stormwarning.co.uk**.

Remember – play harmonica with your ears...

The blues has always been a music passed down from player to player, rather than written down by composers. You can write out blues songs, but you cannot capture what they are about unless you hear them. For example, playing Son House's song "Death Letter" by reading the music will never help you to understand the power of hearing him perform it.

This book is really only a starter, to help you understand how the harmonica works and give you some idea of how to play what you hear. Really, like the Sonnys and Walters that made the harp great, you are on your own and you have to find your own way of playing by listening and learning from records and, if you are lucky, hearing a great harp player like Carey Bell perform live.

So keep your ears open, take a harp with you wherever you go, and have fun exploring the blues. Because the blues will get you someday, and you better be good and ready...

Further playing

Instructional books

The Complete Harmonica Player

This great introduction to the harmonica focuses on the three most popular styles: blues, folk and country. Choose your favorite style to sound like Sonny Boy Williamson, John Mayall or Bob Dylan!
Written by Stuart "Son" Maxwell

Order No. AM 977438

Blues Harp From Scratch – Blues Harmonica For Absolute Beginners

This user-friendly CD-guidebook by Mick Kinsella includes all your favorite tunes such as "Amazing Grace" and "Oh Susanna," plus guidance on note-bending, blues riffs, wah-wah, note splitting, as well as loads of blues solos!

Order No. AM 92630

Songbooks

Bob Dylan For Harmonica

30 great songs – 24 for both diatonic and chromatic harmonica players, six for chromatic only. Includes: "Blowing In The Wind," "Just Like A Woman" and "Under Your Spell."

Order No. AM 932140

DVD

Beginning Blues Harp With Don Baker

Renowned blues harmonica hero Don Baker teaches you how to play this versatile instrument from scratch. You will discover how to bend notes and achieve triplet-tonguing and expressive tone control. Also features a booklet of easy-to-follow notated examples.

Order No. DV 10241N

www.musicsales.com

Track listing and about the CD

The CD included contains spoken instructions and demonstrations to help you learn; it's like having your very own teacher! It demonstrates what the various techniques are supposed to sound like so you can listen carefully and match them up with your own playing. The CD also contains full demonstrations of all pieces with a real live band, plus backing tracks *without* the harmonica, so you can jam along with the band on your own. The first time you hear the piece, it will be the full demonstration, the second time will be the backing track only.

Have fun!

Track	
1	Introduction
2	Get playing

Lesson 1 – Learning to play
3	Holding the harmonica
4	Blowing and drawing
5-6	The Two-Timing Blues
7	Single notes
8	Single note C
9	Bending and wailing
10-11	The One-Note Wail

Lesson 2 – Cross harp
12	Cross harp
13	C scale with guitar C chord
14	Bluesy scale in C with guitar C chord
15-16	The Unblues
17-18	The Cross Harp Blues

Lesson 3 – Wah-wah
19	Wah-wah
20	Wah-wah on hole 4
21-22	The Crying Blues
23-24	The Fox Chase Blues

Lesson 4 – Riffing the blues
25	Riffing the blues
26-27	The Hoodoo Blues
28	Introduction to "Tumblin' Blues"
29-30	Tumblin' Blues

Lesson 5 – Chords and effects
31	The rooster
32-33	Rooster Blues
34	The train
35-36	Train Gone Blues
37	The trill
38-39	Chicago Blues

Lesson 6 – Good vibes
40	Vibrato
41	Tremolo
42-43	The Moody Blues

Lesson 7 – Blow away your blues
44	Improvisation
45-46	City Blues Jam
47-48	Midnight Blues Jam
49-50	Swinging Blues Jam
51-52	Rocking Blues Jam
53	Last word

To remove your CD from the plastic sleeve, lift the small lip to break the perforations.
Replace the disc after use for convenient storage.